Animal  Lives

OWLS

Sally Morgan

QED Publishing

QED

First published in the UK in 2006 by
QED Publishing
A Quarto Group company
226 City Road
London EC1V 2TT

www.qed-publishing.co.uk

A Catalogue record for this book is
available from the British Library.

ISBN 1 84538 378 8

Written by Sally Morgan
Designed by Jonathan Vipond
Editor Hannah Ray
Picture Researcher Joanne Forrest Smith

Publisher Steve Evans
Art Director Zeta Davies
Editorial Director Jean Coppendale

Printed and bound in China

Picture Credits

Key: t=top, b=bottom, l=left, r=right,
c=centre, FC=front cover

Ardea/M Watson 28–29; **Corbis**/Ron
Austing/FLPA 22, /Frank Blackburn/Ecoscene
12, /Martin Harvey 1, /George McCarthy 27,
/Joe McDonald 11, /W Perry Conway 19tr;
Ecoscene/Peter Cairns 24–25, /Fritz Polking
7, /John Pitcher 17tr; **FLPA**/15, /Richard
Brooks 18–19, 30br, /Michael Callan 30tl,
/Paul Hobson 30tr, /Michio Hoshino/Minden
Pictures 23, /Derek Middleton 10, /Malcolm
Schuyl 6, /John Tinning 29tr, /Winfried
Wisniewski/Foto Natura 16–17; **Getty
Images**/Gary Meszaros FC; **NHPA**/ Anthony
Bannister 20, /John & Sue Buckingham 14,
/Jordi bas Casas 8–9, /Manfred Danegger 4,
/Karl Switak 21; **Still Pictures**/C Allan Morgan
9tr, /Hans Pfletschinger 13, /Ed Reschke 5,
/Cal Vornberger 26.

explained in the
Glossary on page 31.

Contents

Owls

The barn owl is one of the best-known owls in the world.

Many people will have heard the sound of an owl hooting at night, but it is unusual to see an owl in the wild. This is because most owls fly at night.

Owls are a type of bird. Birds are animals that are covered in feathers, have wings and lay eggs. Most birds build nests and can fly.

Appearance

Owls are closely related to **birds of prey** such as eagles and falcons. They perch upright and have a large, round head, a short tail, a hooked beak and powerful claws called talons. Male and female owls look alike, but females are often larger.

The great horned owl is named after the tufts of feathers on its ears.

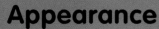

Owl
Owls are often linked with wisdom, but in some countries they are also associated with trickery and evil.
fact

5

Owl types

There are about 200 **species** of owls. They are divided into two groups: barn owls and true owls.

The heart-shaped face is clearly visible on this barn owl.

Barn owls

Barn owls have a heart-shaped face and long legs. Their feathers are generally pale in colour. The middle toe of a barn owl has a special claw which it uses to comb its feathers.

True owls

True owls vary in size. They have a big head with large, round eyes. Their face is round and some have tufts of feathers at the tips of their ears. Usually their legs are covered in feathers. In true owls, the innermost toe is shorter than the middle toe.

Verreaux's eagle owl, an African species, is one of the world's largest owls.

Owl

At 71cm tall, the world's largest owl is the Eurasian eagle owl. The smallest, at just 14cm, is the pygmy owl.

fact

7

Where do you find owls?

Owls are found all over the world except in Antarctica, parts of Greenland and some smaller islands.

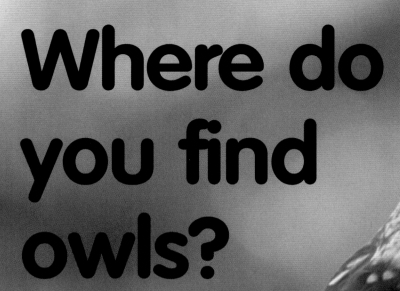

Tengmalm's owl lives in Arctic forest areas.

Owl habitats

Owls are found in many different **habitats**. Most owls prefer woodlands and forests, where there are plenty of nesting sites. However, the snowy owl is found on the icy **tundra** of the far north, and the tiny elf owl survives in the hot deserts of North America. Other species of owl live on grasslands and marshes or on farmland. Some owls live close to people in buildings and gardens. In America, eastern screech owls can even be found in parts of New York.

Snowy owls are found mainly in the Arctic.

Owl fact

The largest-ever owl lived several million years ago. It was over 1m tall and had powerful claws for hunting.

9

Owl nests

Male and female owls often stay together for a long time, and use the same nest year after year. Some owls' nests have been used for more than 20 years.

Barn owls like to nest on ledges inside large buildings, such as barns.

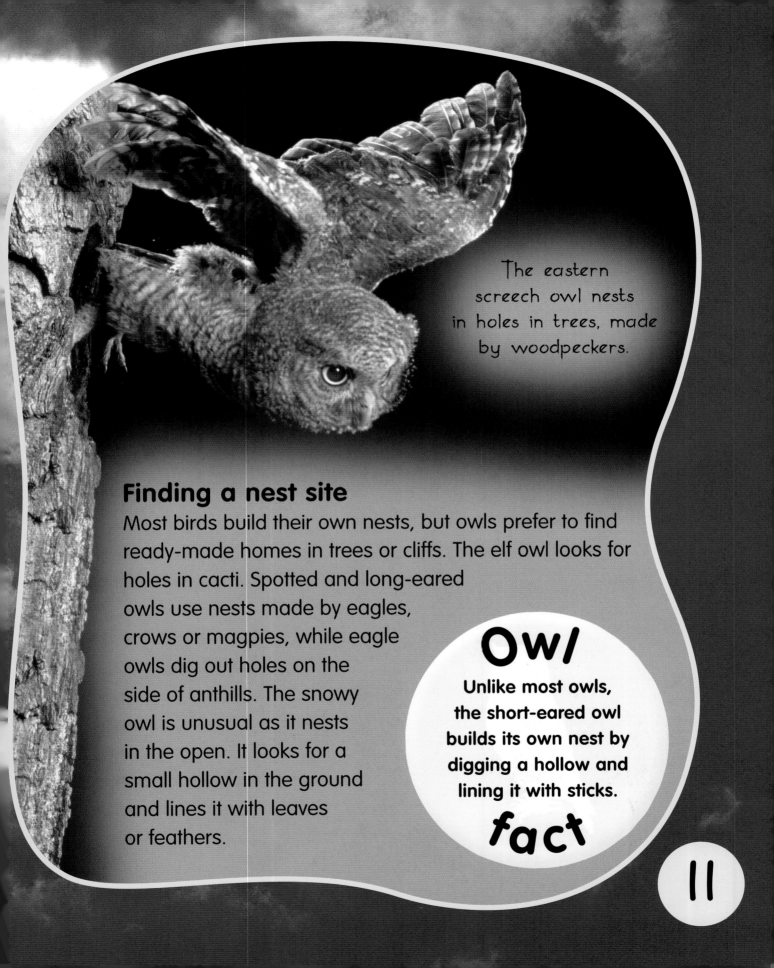

The eastern screech owl nests in holes in trees, made by woodpeckers.

Finding a nest site

Most birds build their own nests, but owls prefer to find ready-made homes in trees or cliffs. The elf owl looks for holes in cacti. Spotted and long-eared owls use nests made by eagles, crows or magpies, while eagle owls dig out holes on the side of anthills. The snowy owl is unusual as it nests in the open. It looks for a small hollow in the ground and lines it with leaves or feathers.

Owl
Unlike most owls, the short-eared owl builds its own nest by digging a hollow and lining it with sticks.
fact

Laying eggs

This long-eared owl is looking after her chicks while the male hunts for food.

Male and female owls breed once a year. After mating, the female lays her eggs every other day for up to two weeks. During a typical breeding season, a female may lay anything from two to seven eggs, depending on how much food she has to eat.

After laying her eggs, the mother owl sits on them for between four and five weeks to **incubate** them before the chicks are ready to hatch out. During this time, she never leaves the nest and is fed by the male owl.

Owl chicks are born with a covering of soft, fluffy feathers. The oldest here is on the left and the youngest on the right.

Large and small

The chicks hatch out one by one. Sometimes it can take as long as two weeks before all the chicks have hatched. This means that the first chick to hatch is larger than the others and gets more of the food. In a good year, all the chicks will survive, but in a poor year the first chick to hatch has the best chance of survival.

Owl

In a good year, the female snowy owl can lay as many as 14 eggs.

fact

Growing up

Owl chicks grow quickly. Their parents take great care of them and bring a constant supply of insects and small animals for the chicks to eat. Some chicks need to be kept warm, so the mother stays close to them until they have grown their feathers.

At about seven weeks, these barn owl chicks will start to grow their adult feathers.

Leaving the nest

As the nest becomes more crowded, the chicks spread their wings and hop onto nearby branches to be fed. At between six and eight weeks old, they are ready to fly away and leave the nest. The young owls often look paler in colour than the adults, with different markings.

Some families stay together even after the chicks have learned to fly. The young of the Pels fishing owl stay close to the nest for as long as eight months.

These young elf owls have now outgrown their nest in a cactus plant.

Flying

Owls are skilled fliers and use their broad wings to soar effortlessly through the air. Unlike many birds, they can slow their flight while they hunt for small animals on the ground below. However, they can also fly quickly. A great horned owl can reach speeds of 60km/h or more.

The snowy owl flies in daylight, making short trips from perch to perch.

Silent flight

Most birds make a flapping noise when they fly, caused by the air rushing over the surface of their wings. Owls' wings are different. The soft feathers at the front edge of their wings muffle the sound and allow the owls to swoop silently down on their **prey**.

This well-**camouflaged** scops owl hunts at night and sits in trees during the day.

Moulting

Over time, an owl's feathers gradually become damaged and worn, so once a year the old feathers drop out and new ones grow in their place. This is called **moulting**. Some birds moult all their feathers at the same time, but owls only lose two or three feathers at a time.

Owl

Some owls that hunt at night use camouflage to blend in with their surroundings while they rest during the day.

fact

Owl senses

Owls are famous for their sharp eyesight and for being able to see in poor light. An owl cannot move its eyes in their sockets, so it has to swivel its whole head in order to look around.

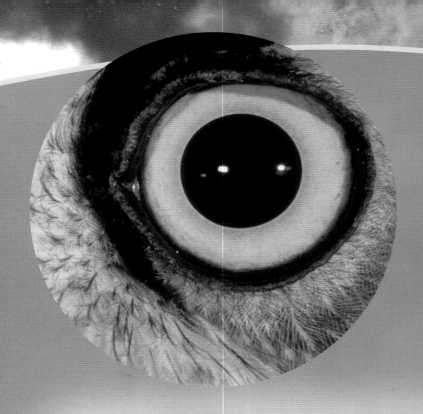

The pupil is the dark spot in the middle of the eye that lets in light.

This short-eared owl relies on its hearing to find voles, which are its favourite prey.

Owl

A great grey owl can hear a beetle running through the grass up to 30m away.

fact

Listening in the dark

Owls have good hearing, too. They can hunt in total darkness, using sounds to find and catch their prey. The way the feathers are arranged on the owl's face helps to funnel sounds towards its ears.

In barn owls, one ear is slightly higher than the other. This means that sounds reach one ear a little before the other. By turning its head, the owl can locate the source of the sound with pinpoint accuracy.

Feeding

Owls are **carnivores** and feed on animals such as insects, birds and small **mammals** including voles, mice and rabbits. The Pels fishing owl eats fish, while some of the larger owls may even eat smaller species of owl.

This Pels fishing owl has caught a fish.

Pellets

Owls swallow their food whole, including any fur and feathers. Six to seven hours later, they cough up the **indigestible** parts in the form of a pellet, which they drop on the ground. Owl pellets are like shiny black sausages about the size of a man's thumb.

Owl fact

The Pels fishing owl has tiny bristles on its claws to help it to grip slippery fish.

By examining pellets, scientists can discover what the owl has been eating.

Hunting

A saw whet owl catches its prey in its outstretched talons.

Owls that live in forests or woods hunt in a different way from owls that live in open habitats. Woodland owls sit still in the treetops, watching and listening for small animals moving on the ground below. As soon as they spot their prey, they launch themselves from their branch and swoop down to snatch their victim.

This snowy owl has carried its prey back to the nest to feed its young.

The search for prey

Owls that live in open habitats such as grassland, farmland or desert, fly slowly over the ground, looking for small animals. Sometimes they will criss-cross the same piece of land again and again to make sure they do not miss their prey.

Territories

Most owls live in a particular **territory** where they have their nest, rear their young and catch their food. Some owls will even defend their territory from other birds of the same species.

The size of an owl's territory varies, depending on what it eats and how much food it can catch. A great horned owl needs up to 350 **hectares**, while a great grey owl can manage with just 100 square metres, as long as food is plentiful.

Migrating owls

Not all owls live in the same place all the
year round. Some **migrate** between winter
and summer feeding areas. However,
unlike other birds, owls do not migrate
every year but only when they cannot
find enough food to eat.

Tawny owls live in the same place
all the year round. Their territory can
range in size from 12 to 100 hectares.

Owl
The short-eared owl
may fly up to 2000km
between its winter and
summer homes.
fact

Communication

The hooting of an owl is a spooky sound. Not all owls are able to make sounds, but most owls hoot to communicate with each other at night.

Owls can also shriek, bark and even sing. They are particularly noisy in the weeks before the breeding season.

Screech owls are named after the loud screech they make when attacked.

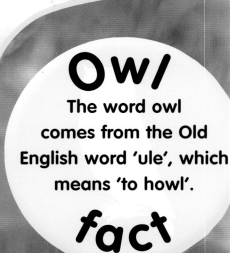

Hooting owls

The tawny owl is particularly well known for its song which sounds like 'to-woo' or sometimes 'hoooouh-ho, hohohohoooouh'. The sound carries a long way at night and is often answered by another owl. Some pairs of screech owls sing together, with the male and female taking it in turns to complete the song.

The burrowing owl has a rattling call that sounds like the warning sounds produced by a rattlesnake. This keeps **predators** away.

Owls under threat

All around the world, owls are under threat.
The main cause is the destruction of their
habitat, as forests are cleared for timber
or new farmland.

Many owls are poisoned by chemicals
which farmers use to protect their
crops. When the owls eat rats, mice
and other animals that have been
killed by pesticides, they too become
poisoned and die. Owls are also
under threat because some people
steal owls' eggs, even though it is
illegal in many countries. This means
the eggs never hatch and the owl
population declines.

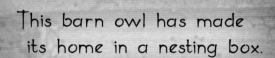

This barn owl has made
its home in a nesting box.

28

Owls may lose their nesting sites when trees are felled.

Saving owls

Fortunately, owls are popular birds and many people are working to save them. Some of the most important habitats for owls have been made into nature reserves so that they are protected. In some places, people are building special boxes so that owls have plenty of sites in which to nest.

Owl

Of the 26 threatened owl species, 4 are facing **extinction**, including the Seychelles scops owl and the forest owlet.

fact

Newly hatched chicks in nest

Older chicks

Life cycle

A female owl can lay eggs when she is 1 year old. Once a year, she lays between 2 and 7 eggs, which take 4 to 5 weeks to hatch. Both parents look after the chicks. Young owls leave their parents after 2 to 8 months. The life span of an owl varies. Small species only live for 2 to 3 years, but larger species live much longer. In the wild, a barn owl will only live for about 2 years, but in captivity they can live for as long as 34 years.

Adult barn owl

Glossary

birds of prey birds such as eagles and falcons that hunt and eat small animals

camouflage when the colouring of an owl's feathers helps it to blend in with its surroundings

carnivore an animal that eats meat

extinction when a species no longer exists

habitat place where an animal or plant lives

hectare area equal to 10 000 square metres

incubate to keep eggs warm until they are ready to hatch

indigestible unable to be broken down and pass through an owl's body

mammal animal that produces milk to feed its young

migration a journey a bird or other animal makes from its winter to summer feeding or breeding grounds

moulting when an owl replaces old or damaged feathers with new ones

predator an animal that hunts other animals

prey an animal that is hunted by other animals

species group of animals that look alike and can produce young together

territory area where an owl nests, rears its young and hunts for food

tundra large frozen region around the North Pole where no trees grow

Index